THE NEVER-ENDING SUN

John Birdsall

John Birdsall
33 Wavendon House Drive
Lower End Road
Wavendon
MK17 8AG

A CIP catalogue record for this book is available from the British Library.

ISBN 1873475 15 2

Printed and bound in Great Britain.

For my Mum -
who is fighting cancer and winning!

Acknowledgements

Among the hundreds of requests I made for money, products and help there was a small number of people who had the balls to say yes. I'd like to thank them not just for their help but for their faith in me. It is thanks to them that I got to the starting point.

My financial sponsors were: IMSI (UK) Ltd, Executive Property Services Ltd, Drummond Sharp Fuel Oil and Lubricant Sales, Icelandair, Ground Modelling Systems Ltd, and MGH Shipping.

Yet more people gave their time during the planning stage for sponsorship, contacts, advise, and simply to help. My special thanks to: Mark Connolly, Steve Bull, Fay Hercod, Wavendon Golf Club, Barry Birdsall, Paul Birdsall, Jan Birdsall, Lynne and Dave Culliton, Paul Everns, Jeanette Fickert, Mike Paul, Jill Barby, Ian and Sara Livemore

Special thanks to my patron, Ffyona Campbell, for believing in me and for being there.

I would like to thank my Mum, Jan Birdsall, for her help in editing this book.

In Iceland, I would like to send my thanks to Baldvin Bjornsson, his wife Sigrun and family, and Baldvin's army of friends who helped us to get across Iceland and to the end. We would not have got there without you!

And last but not least, my very deepest thanks to those who were on the road with me, my back-up crew: John Sheeran, Dianne Benson, Andrea Aborn, and Stuart Edwards. If I hadn't had good people who went that extra mile for me, I would still be sitting in a corner staring at a wall.

CHEERS TEAM!
John Birdsall

Foreword

I offer my congratulations to John and his back-up crew for completing their aim. Despite serious obstacles in their way they found answers to almost every problem that this kind of journey would throw at them.

If you have any desire to travel or fulfil a dream, this book will inspire you to get up and do it!

Many professional adventurers and explorers think that going on an expedition with disabled people is impractical and dangerous. John has proved that this is not necessarily so.

Ffyona Campbell

Iceland is Europe's second largest island (Britain is the largest).

Iceland lies 400 miles from Scotland and 240 miles from Greenland (its nearest neighbour) and, with the exception of the island of Grimsey and a few small rocks, Iceland lies completely south of the Arctic Circle.

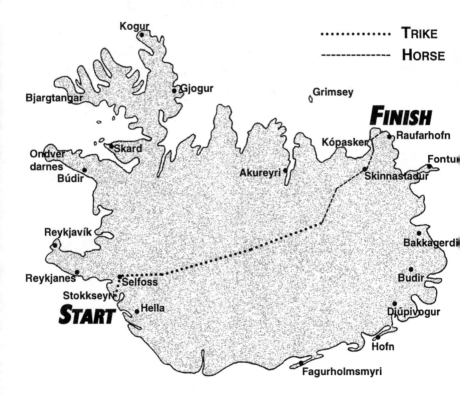

I did a total of 304 miles. Of that I did 180 miles on the trike and 124 miles on horseback.

Chapter One

I was sitting on my trike with my left foot in the Atlantic Ocean - waiting to start my journey across Iceland, diagonally from south west to north east. The trek would finish at the Arctic Ocean some 300 miles away.

I was using a small petrol-driven trike with a top speed of 5mph (walking speed). This trike, which was designed for disabled people, had taken me from Land's End to John O' Groats in 1993.

I am myself disabled, I have cerebral palsy. I cannot walk or talk. I use an electronic communicator to talk with and an electric wheelchair to get around.

After seven months of fundraising and planning, I found myself on another crazy expedition, accompanied by a back-up crew travelling in a Land Rover. On the journey ahead, they will meet me every five miles (an hour's drive on the trike). Ahead of us lay Sprengisandur, a track that runs through Europe's largest desert, just under 200 miles of desolate rough terrain, black sand, lava, unbridged rivers and rocks.

Seven months earlier, Christmas Day 1994. *One Foot in the Grave* on TV, and me wondering what this pile of crap was doing on the television and what the hell I was doing watching it. Last year I had trekked the length of the UK, I'd been to Iceland before; so, O.K., let's trike across Iceland.

One night in January 95, I took Chris, my helper, out for a pizza. He was leaving to travel round New Zealand for three months. I got in at 9.45 and was just thinking of going for a pint when I turned on the TV. Ffyona Campbell appeared on the screen and I was glued to the spot. What she was doing and what she was saying about it were things I could really relate to. Next morning I received my regular listing of talks at the Royal Geographical Society. I opened it half asleep - and there she was again: Ffyona Campbell, talking about her walk. I booked a ticket. I then went into town and found myself in W.H. Smiths looking for a birthday present. There she was again: Ffyona Campbell, *On Foot Through Africa*. I forgot about the birthday present and bought the book!

In February I wrote to Ffyona, then met her at her flat in London a week later. We got on well, we were on the same wavelength, we knew what each other was on about straightaway. It was like a breath of fresh air.

The expedition suddenly took off. A trike ride from the south to the north was the aim. I wrote to John and Cean Sheeran, two brothers who had come with me on my last trip to Iceland, to see if they wanted to be part of the expedition. 'Yes, great idea, count us in,' they replied.

The next month I wrote the Bullshit sheet and put a budget together. I asked Icelandair for free flights to Iceland. A guy who I met in my local pub, Mark Connolly, said that his computer software company might be able to sponsor the lot: £5000. I got pissed that night! Mark phoned next day saying, 'can't make £5000, but we can do £1000, will that do?'

'Yes, that's better than sod all!'

Mark's interest in the trip made working with him really good. We kept in touch through faxes and meetings down the pub. I asked Ffyona if she would like to be the expedition's patron. 'Yes,' she said, 'I am flattered to be asked, thank you.'

I'd put an advert in the Royal Geographical Society magazine and a letter soon arrived from a girl in Wales, Dianne Benson. Dianne was interested in joining the expedition and came to meet me three weeks later. We got on well, but she made a mistake by saying that she was a trained cook! I put Dianne in charge of the expedition's food.

I hadn't heard from John and Cean so I phoned them. 'Oh, is it on then, JB?' (I was known to most of my friends as JB, this was handy because we had two John's in the team!) 'I thought it was just an idea.'

'No, John,' I said, 'it is on. I have got two grand and a Land Rover ready.'

'I don't think we can make it, money problems, I'll try to get some people for you.' Three days later Cean phoned. 'I've found a girl who is interested in joining you, can I bring her up next week to meet you?' This was Andrea; she was from New Zealand and had been to Iceland before building paths. She did not say much, but she seemed at home with Iceland and the outdoors.

So that was two girls, but I needed some muscles. A week later Andrea phoned, she had been in touch with a bloke, Dave, who was interested in joining the team. I spoke to Dave a few times on the phone. On the third call we had a misunderstanding. He got annoyed so I sacked him. I then phoned John and told him that there was a place on the trip for him, if he changed his mind. One hour later he phoned. 'Yes, I want to go, is that alright?' Then, finally, another bloke, called Trevor, came to see me. He was very keen to be on the trip, perhaps a little too keen.

The press day was booked at the Royal Geographical Society on the 27th of June. The Land Rover was booked on the ferry to Iceland on the 29th, and the flights for the 4th of July.

Chapter Two

June was quite a month! Everything was happening. Phone calls, faxes flying about in all directions - I ran out of fax paper twice that month! John was now going to film the trip and we had many late night conversations about the angle the trip should be filmed from. Some very weird ideas came out of those calls.

On the 1st of June we still did not have a Land Rover, we had been let down by two garages. By the 8th of June I decided to try and get a loan to hire a Land Rover. Time was short. The trip couldn't go ahead without a Land Rover, and Icelandair were nagging me about the £800 for the flights. If I cancelled the flights because of lack of back-up transport, I wouldn't see my £800 again. On the 19th of June I hired a Land Rover for eight weeks at the cost of £2000. Then Icelandair got their £800. The expedition was on, there was no backing out now!

Dianne arrived on the 22nd to buy, sort out and pack the food for the four week expedition. She had two days to do it in as the rest of the team were coming to pack the Land Rover. My flat was covered with boxes of food, camping gear and spares for my trike. My neighbours did not know what the hell was happening when tents started to go up in my garden; people were going around in a state of panic swearing constantly. I asked John to phone Trevor to ask why he couldn't make it on the day we were packing the Land Rover. This was an important day because this was the first time I had managed to get the team together in one place! But then John phoned me back. 'JB, Trevor has dropped out.' Cean said he had no work on; he could take Trevor's place if I wanted him to. 'Yes, I would like that,' I said.

The next day we had the Anglia News film crew over, they did some tracking shots of me on the trike and interviewed me and John (we gave some naff answers). After that we had our press day at the Royal Geographical Society. A radio station asked us to do a live radio interview by phone at 9am that morning. John and I sat in my kitchen drinking coffee at 8am trying to get it together. The radio station had faxed the questions the night before and I pre-programmed my communicator with my answers. The dreaded 'WHY' question was there! I pre-programmed the answer: 'I don't know, but I'll tell you when I get back, maybe it's the challenge that I like'.

We then drove into London with the full kit, the loaded Land Rover, trailer and the trike, and parked it in the garden of the Royal Geographical Society. It was a hot day. Ffyona arrived and we gave a few radio interviews. My Mum, sister and brother were there, not many press arrived but we had a great day.

Two days later John called. 'JB, Cean cannot go to Iceland, his girlfriend won't let him go!' I was not in the mood to ask why. John said, 'I was talking to Andrea's boyfriend, Stuart, at the press day, he seemed OK. He is an ex-army mechanic, do you want me to ask him?'

'Yes, OK,' I said. Ten minutes later John rang back.

'Yes, he would love to go.'

'God,' I said, 'I hope that one day someone asks me on a expedition with three day's notice when all the hard work has been done!'

4th July, the big day. We got up at 10am feeling confident. A good luck fax came from Ffyona saying she wished she was coming too. A spare communicator arrived through the post: Christ, that came just in time! I was just packing my film when my Mum and Dad rang to ask me out to lunch. I got back at 2pm and we needed to leave for Heathrow at 4pm. Dianne went to Tesco's to get some bits for the first aid kit and some food for my cat. Then I recorded a message on my answering machine: 'This is John Birdsall. I have gone for a ride on my trike.'

Dianne and I got to Heathrow at 5pm and went to the bar. At 6.15pm the rest of the team arrived. I said my first hello to Stuart, he was a typical army type, with tattoos and a bald head. I looked at John, John raised one eyebrow at me, then we checked in. We were soon in the air, banking over London to head north. 70 percent of the planes taking off from Heathrow head south, but we went the opposite way! It was midnight when we landed in Iceland two and a half hours later, and we were greeted by heavy wind and rain.

Our first problem was where to stay that night until we could pick up the Land Rover at 9am the next morning. We thought that we'd try to stay in the airport until early morning, then get the bus into Reykjavik at about 7am. Kelfavik is Iceland's International Airport, it is about a 45 minute drive from Iceland's capital, Reykjavik. It may be an International Airport but it's a quiet one, especially at one in the morning. We couldn't hide in the crowd. There were no lounges, not even a coffee machine; this could be a long night. We got settled in a corridor. Staring out of the window at the horrific weather, John said, 'JB, your next trip is going to be to Jamaica.' Jamaica, Mmmmmm.

Just as we were getting 'comfortable', a official looking Icelandic girl walked by and said 'You're not allowed to stay here overnight.' It was that 'not allowed' bit I didn't like, it reminded me of school. We argued with her for about five minutes before giving up, we were not getting anywhere.

It was still raining when we got on the bus to Reykjavik, and fairly dark, which was strange for Iceland at this time of year. The bus dumped us at Reykjavik's internal airfield. We plunged ourselves and all our gear in the foyer to see if we got kicked out again but no one took any notice. By this time we were getting very knackered and it was a relief to stretch out. Dianne got some sandwiches out. John starting eating one, then slowly looked up and said in a soft voice with a pained expression, 'Dianne, what's in this sandwich?'

'Oh, I made them up with what was left in JB's fridge as we left, it's cheese and peanut butter,' said Dianne. John looked at her in disbelief, then looked at the half-eaten sandwich and said, 'I am eating a cheese and peanut butter sandwich at four in the morning!'

At 7am the airport cafe opened. Icelanders treat their coffee seriously, it is always percolated and served in a flask. Once you've paid, you can have as many refills as you want. This is how Icelanders stay awake during the long days of their summer! After about an hour, we were slowly waking up.

By 10am we got our Land Rover from Customs without any real hassle. Then we were heading out of Reykjavik south east to Selfoss where we camped. It was cold and raining. I was really cold, shit, I thought, have I brought enough jumpers? I couldn't remember being this cold on my last trip. Perhaps it was because I was so knackered. We slept for a couple of hours, ate, then decided to go for a ride to Skogafoss: a 62 m high waterfall. On the way back the rain had stopped, the clouds parted to reveal a clear blue sky. I looked at my watch, it was a quarter past twelve in the morning. I was on an expedition in Iceland again, doing stupid things at stupid times. It felt excellent.

Chapter Three

Iceland's first inhabitants were Irish monks, who regarded the island as a sort of hermitage until the early 9th century. They were followed by Iceland's first permanent settlers, who came from Norway. This was Iceland's Age of Settlement, traditionally defined as the period between 870 and 930AD, when political strife on the Scandinavian mainland caused many to flee.

Having just escaped political turbulence in Scandinavia, Iceland's settlers were in no mood for a monarchy and developed a parliamentary system of government. A district assembly and Althing (National Assembly) were founded, and a code of law prepared. Iceland became a Christian country in 999, which engendered some semblance of national unity at a time when squabbles were arising among its leaders and allegiances were being questioned. The country flourished during the next century, and established a thriving agrarian economy with little unrest.

Iceland then became a launching pad for explorations of the North Atlantic: Eric the Red, who grew up in Iceland as the son of a Norwegian exile, colonised Greenland in 982;

and Eric's Icelandic son, Leif Eriksson, is widely thought to have been the first European to explore the coast of North America - which he named Vinland the Good. One of the more reliable Icelandic sagas, however, suggests that Leif Eriksson learned of Vinland from another Icelander, Bjarni Herjulfsson, who had been there some fourteen years earlier. Whatever the truth is, these voyages of exploration became the source material of one of Europe's great literary flowerings.

The first literary tradition to emerge was poetry, which tended to be heroic in theme. Poetry was displaced during the Saga Age of the late 12th to late 13th centuries, when epic and dramatic tales of early settlement, romance, dispute and the development of Iceland were recorded. These provided both a sense of cultural heritage for Icelandic commoners and entertaining yarns on the bitterly cold winter nights.

By the early 13th century, two hundred years of peace and literary development came to an end. The country entered the infamous Sturlung Age, a turbulent era of political treachery and violence. The opportunistic Norwegian King Hákon Hákonarson promptly stepped in, and Iceland became a Norwegian province, to be plundered mercilessly. To add insult to injury, the volcano Mt Hekla erupted in 1300, 1341 and 1389, causing widespread death and destruction. Recurring epidemics also plagued the country, and the Black Death that struck Norway in 1349 effectively cut off trade and supplies.

At the end of the 14th century, Iceland was brought under Danish rule. After the Reformation of 1550 Lutheranism was adopted as the country's religion. Throughout the next two centuries, Iceland was crippled by rampant Danish profiteering, beset by international pirates and subject to an increasing number of natural disasters.

Denmark's grip on Iceland was broken in 1874 when Iceland drafted a constitution and was permitted to handle its own domestic matters. Iceland was released from Danish rule in 1918, making it an independent state within the Kingdom of Denmark, with Copenhagen retaining responsibility for defence and foreign affairs. However, in 1940 Denmark was occupied by Germany. Iceland realised that the Kingdom was in no position to continue overseeing its affairs and, a year later, requested independence. It was granted on the 17th of June 1944.

After the occupation of Denmark and Iceland's declaration of sovereignty, the island's vulnerability became a matter of concern for the Allied powers. British and US troops were moved in. The Americans still remain, much to the chagrin of a growing number of Icelanders who want them out. The Brits incurred Icelandic wrath when they refused to recognise Iceland's expanded territorial fishing rights in the 1970s. For a few years, clashes between Icelandic gunships and British warships during the so-called Cod Wars became a regular feature of the fishing season.

Iceland is currently in a situation of economic decline, and the country is becoming increasingly indebted as the fishing industry languishes. Fishing quotas have been cut back, unemployment has risen and the króna devalued. Clashes between environmental organisations and the Icelandic whaling industry, which split from the International Whaling Commission in 1992, also hasn't helped matters. On a brighter note, while natural disasters continue to occur, better communications and a more urban population have reduced their impact considerably.

The Presidency of Iceland was implemented on June 17th, 1944, Independence Day, when

Mr Sveinn Björnsson was sworn into office. The Presidency of Iceland is a non-political office that has limited power over domestic issues (the president can refuse to sign laws but has only once done so, and then delayed signing only for one day). The office is similar to the royalties of Europe when it comes to actual day-to-day power.

Iceland's Scandinavian-type economy is basically capitalistic, but has an extensive welfare system, relatively low unemployment, and comparatively even distribution of income. The economy is heavily dependent on the fishing industry, which provides 78.7 percent (1993) of export earnings and employs 12 percent of the workforce. In the absence of other natural resources - except energy - Iceland's economy is vulnerable to changing world fish prices, and has been in recession since 1988.

The center-right government's economic goals include reducing the budget and current account deficits, limiting foreign borrowing, containing inflation, revising agricultural and fishing policies, diversifying the economy, and privatising state-owned industries. The recession has led to a wave of bankruptcies and mergers throughout the economy, as well as the highest unemployment of the post-World War II period

(4.8% in 1994). Inflation, previously a serious problem, declined from double digit rates in the 1980s to only 3.7% in 1992-93.

* * *

The next day we looked for a place where we could get the trike down to the Atlantic for the start of the trek, and chose a spot at Eyarbakki a few miles south of Selfoss. The final route plan for the trek looked simple enough. We thought we'd be able to crack it in three weeks, no problem, leaving a week left for a holiday - but don't tell the sponsors!

We packed up camp the next day and headed for the start point. The trike was unloaded while I put on my over-trousers and a jacket. I wore my over- trousers all the time on the trek, they kept the wind and rain out as well as keeping my trousers clean. I liked kneeling, being mobile on my knees during rest stops. I rode down a rocky path and onto the beach, reversed the back wheels into the sea and killed the engine. After a five minute photo session I plunged my left foot into the sea, restarted the trike and eased out of the sea. The trek had begun. I hate starts.

I got onto the road and left the team to catch up. After two miles the trike was going well and I began to relax. The Land Rover came past and slowed in front. John was sitting cross legged in the back of the trailer filming me. After about a mile they went off and waited at the first five mile rest stop. The road was being resurfaced: too late guys, I'm here already!

I saw the Land Rover up ahead, tea was on the go. I had noticed there were no lights working on the trailer; closer inspection showed that all the wires to the lights had some how been cut and they were dragging on the road. I left them fixing it.

The next five miles took us through Selfoss and onto Road 1. The Land Rover drove behind me through the town and for about two miles after that, then went onto the next road stop to make lunch. Road 1 goes all around Iceland and is prettybusy, but after the Land's End to John O' Groats trip it was a piece of cake. I will never forget the A30 out of Cornwall and Devon!

I finally spotted the Land Rover parked in a hotel car park, I had done 15 miles. Lunch time. I was planning to do 30 miles a day, 15 miles before lunch and 15miles after, with six rest stops. This worked out at about eight hours on the road each day.

The weather changes suddenly in Iceland. The air is so clear that when the sun is out it is red hot but the next minute it can turn freezing. I was to continue on road 1 but not for long, we were looking for a left turn, road 30, which will take us into the desert. We had planned to reach the desert in two day's time, and then the real expedition would start.

It was exactly five miles from where we had lunch to the left turn to road 30. The Land Rover was parked at a petrol station next to the turning. John was on the roof of the Land Rover filming me as I pulled off road 1 and into the station. I felt OK so I carried on for another five miles along the quieter road 30, I felt I was getting somewhere now once I had left road 1 behind. After 27 miles I saw the Land Rover pull in at a campsite, I was all set to stop for the night as well. We had done well, we did not start until late and it was the first day.

Behind the campsite, called Brautarholt, loomed Hekla, the volcano which erupted three years ago. The team started to settle down. There was a bad vibe between John and Dianne and Stuart and Andrea. Stuart and Andrea were a couple; he was ex-army and a know-all, she was a bit of a wet fart, but so far I had got on OK with them. I had been on a expedition with

John before, I liked him a lot. John was solid, he knew what he liked in life and what he didn't. Dianne was the best expeditioner on the team. She said what she thought and didn't give a shit what she said, she also had a great sense of humour, which helped. I hoped that they would all settle down.

The next day was to take us to the edge of the desert. Another dry day. As I reached the right turn onto road 32, the signpost said: 32 - to F28 Sprengisandur; F28 being the name of the track that goes through the desert. I got onto road 32 via a cattle grid. The landscape suddenly turned wild. A push bike passed me loaded up with panniers front and back: I was glad not to be the only nutter around. I looked ahead and saw a never-ending straight track. The track was sandy and smooth, the trike went over it well.

A rest stop was due, where the hell is the Land Rover, shit am I on the right track? The track turned into a road again, and I reckoned that I must be heading to a quarry because heavy duty lorries kept passing me. I saw the dust first and about a minute later a lorry would appear and thunder past me. Another minute would go by before could see through all the dust. Luckily at five miles an hour, the trike would not go off course much when I couldn't see!

I saw the Land Rover at the top of this massive steep hill. Half way up the hill the road deteriorated into a very rocky track. I finally reached the Land Rover and had a twenty minute rest.

'How is it out there?' asked Dianne.

'It's starting to get tough.'

'I can smell the desert; it's not far away,' said John.

'Ya.'

Stuart suddenly shouted 'LORRY!', and one thundered past, covering my coffee in dust.

The landscape changed again, green fields with a lake to the left of me. The sun was out and it was getting hot. I climbed a steep hill with some green verges on either side of me. The hill was so steep the trike began to cough, and I was being attacked by hordes of flies. When I reached the top of the hill, the wind got up, which got rid of the flies, and the trike was a bit happier as well. I saw the Land Rover again. Sometimes the five miles passed quickly, butsome were never-ending. We had dinner overlooking the green fields and blue lakes.

Iceland, the second largest island in Europe, boils and splutters in the Atlantic Ocean north-west of Scotland, west of Norway and south-east of Greenland. The main island, which stretches 500km east to west and 300km north to south, is characterised by desert plateaus, sandy deltas, volcanoes, lava fields, and glacial icecaps. Over half the country is above 400 metres, with the highest point, Hvannadalshnúkur, rising 2119 metres above sea-level. Only 21 percent of the land, all near the coast, is considered arable and habitable. The bulk of Iceland's population and agriculture is concentrated in the south-west between Reykjavík and Vík.

Iceland is a relatively young landmass subject to periodic rumpling by volcanic activity. Earthquakes are as exciting as breakfast here, with people only bothering to take notice of big proper explosions, ones that raise up an island where once there was ocean, ones that sculpt the earth anew. It's hardly surprising with all this rumbling, shaking and spouting that the landscape is pretty well devoid of trees (though, in fairness, an ambitious reforestation project means the country now enjoys a few recreational forests and patches of scrubby birch).

What the country does have, however, is large expanses of tundra, grassland, bogs and barren desert. The only indigenous land mammal is the Arctic fox, although polar bears, which occasionally drift across from Greenland on ice floes, would be indigenous if they weren't considered so undesirable. Introduced animals include reindeer, mink and field mice. The country has a wealth of birdlife, especially sea birds, and its seas are rich in marine mammals and fish. Freshwater fish are limited to eels, salmon, trout and Arctic char.

Iceland's southern and western coasts experience relatively mild winter temperatures thanks to the warm waters of the Gulf Stream, though it still tends to rain an awful lot. In January, for instance, Reykjavík enjoys an average of only three sunny days (in July, one fine day is the norm). July and August are the warmest months and, in general, the chances of fine weather improve as you move north and east. It's sunniest around Akureyri and Lake Mývatn in the central north and warmest around Egilsstaoir in the east, yet neither place seems to be free of an uncomfortably cold wind. While they're more prone to clear weather than the coastal areas, the interior deserts can experience other problems such as blizzards and high winds which whip up dust and sand into swirling, gritty maelstroms.

The next five miles seemed very long, then the Land Rover suddenly shot by me. Hey, what's going on, I thought, they should be in front: I saw them pass me ages ago! The Land Rover stopped and John got out. 'Sorry,' he said, 'we went to see a waterfall. We thought we had time but you were too fast for us.'

I had a drink, then got going again. The road barred left up a steep hill then a sharp right up an even steeper one. I still had lorries going past. By now I was climbing high and my ears started to pop. Dust from the lorries was getting beyond a joke. The Land Rover had stopped at the top of the hill overlooking another blue lake. I stopped for a breather. We now had flies as well as dust. Andrea said, 'let's go and find a nice grassy campsite by a river.'

I thought when I left them, what planet was she on? OK, a grassy campsite by a river would be nice but somehow I didn't think there was going to be one around here! Six miles later I saw our little camp, we were in the desert. Stuart helped me down a small sharp bank which got me off the desert track and onto the volcanic black sand where the tents had been pitched. The Land Rover and trailer were parked next to the tents and it looked a great set up from the track. But as soon has I had switched off the trike I realised that we were infested with flies. Swarms of them attacked my face at once. John took off my jacket and chucked it over me. The only thing you can do in those situations is laugh. About twenty minutes later the wind got up which shifted the flies and we had dinner in peace. The sense of peace was amazing. The sun was low, creating massive long shadows across the desert. It was great to be there.

Chapter Four

Before I set off the next morning, Stuart cleaned the air filter on the trike, which was full of shit. It was another dry day, though a bit gloomy and misty: a good atmosphere for my first full day of trekking through the desert. The Land Rover passed me and I was on my own again. We knew there was a road running parallel to me that I would meet soon. That was the F28, the main track running through the desert. No one knew what the 'F' was for at first but after a week of being on this desert track we had our own ideas of what it stood for!

At one point I had to cross a wooden bridge, about 100 feet long with a very long drop to the river below: I was glad to get off it. I got to the crossroad and turned left onto the F28. This is a single-lane track and the only traffic on it, really, are the big 4x4 trucks and tour buses. These buses are not like normal buses! They are built in Iceland to carry tourists from one side of the island to the other, have four-wheel drive, and stand about eight feet off the ground.

Towards the end of the five miles I approached some buildings, one story high but very long. They looked weird just sitting in the middle of nowhere. Then I saw the Land Rover parked alongside them. It was a café - COFFEE! It felt hot inside after being outside for days. The team had been there for a good half hour before me and they were well mellowed out. John was drawing in the visitors' book, one of his drawings of the Land Rover and me on the trike. Time to go before we got too comfortable. I had the luxury of using a real loo before we went.

The trike did not want to start, perhaps it had mellowed out as well! It eventually started after a lot of messing about with the electrics and the air filter. I was on the road again, the Land Rover followed me for a mile just in case the trike gave trouble again, but it was OK. The track turned into a cemented road as it went through an hydro-electric plant then it turned back into a soft track again as it climbed a long steep hill. I was half way up the hill when I discovered that the throttle cable had snapped. The trike was still going flat out. The only way to stop it was to switch the engine off by the ignition, the trike stopped in the middle of the track. I could see the Land Rover parked at the top of the hill. I put my indicator on and hoped they would see I had a problem; they did and came to see what was up.

We got the trike on the side of the track and Stuart started to replace the cable. The trike was about twelve years old. The firm who built it went bust years ago, so getting spares for the trike before the trip was quite a job. I finally got some spare throttle cables from a lawnmower shop. They looked the same as the trike's, but when Stuart was fitting them we discovered they were slightly different. Dianne got a brew on and we drank coffee while Stuart persuaded the throttle cable to fit. I finally got going again. The cable was shorter so we had take the fibreglass flooring off to let the cable run free. With the floor off it looked like a vehicle out of Mad Max, unstoppable! Don't mess with me, I am on a journey - so move out of my way, boy!

Eight miles later I was going up a steep rocky hill when a thought suddenly hit me: FUEL, I cannot remember refuelling today. Thirty seconds later the trike coughed and stopped, after another twenty seconds the rain started. It was not a good day. The team had just gone ahead to set up camp. I had a note in my pocket saying 'I have a problem, please find Land Rover up ahead, thank you' and waited for an unsuspecting vehicle to appear. This turned out to be a bus. It stopped, and an Icelandic girl got out. I chucked her the note. The bus was full of Germans who constantly stared at me, I stared back with my look that said, 'will you please stop staring and get a life.'

The Icelandic girl stayed with me while the driver went to find the Land Rover, which followed him back some time later. Stuart stuck his head out the window, 'what's up?' I pointed to the fuel tank.

'FUEL, FUCK, I bloody knew it, sorry!'

While Stuart was refuelling the trike, he told me that the driver had given him a bollocking for leaving a poor disabled person in the middle of nowhere. I just laughed and restarted the trike.

'The camp is about three miles away,' Stuart said. 'We are on top of a hill, try not to make it four brakedowns in one day!'

'OK,' I replied. I had a good run to the camp. The track was smooth and mostly uphill. I at last reached the camp and the end of the day! The camp had a spectacular view of glaciers, beyond the miles and miles of desert surrounding us. My sister, Lynne was flying to Lansaroti that day, and I was sure that she would not be seeing a view better than this one out of her warm, clean apartment. We had a beer and hoped that Lynne was having as good a time as us in her squeaky clean apartment with a shower and a loo. Sadly we knew that she would not have the excellent feeling we did when we went off into the desert to go to the loo. Squatting and looking around at a panoramic view of nothingness is the most brilliant feeling that most people will never experience!

Chapter Five

We woke up to rain the next morning. It sounded bad in the tent but when we got out and put our waterproofs on it was not too bad. It was a cold day, time for gloves. Me and gloves do not get on, especially my right hand. I use my left hand most of the time and only use my right hand for the one important thing in life, riding my trike! Most of the time my right hand is curled up, so getting a glove on is a laugh especially when it's cold and raining! Dianne and I finally got the glove on while John sat in front of us with the video camera laughing at me and Dianne swearing at a glove. The left glove went on in seconds.

I got on the track and got going, leaving the others to pack up. The rain was fine and light and it was the coldest day on the trek yet. The track was made from smooth black volcanic sand. My second rest stop was at the 90 miles mark. There was a big 90 drawn in the sand on the road. I had a drink of orange to celebrate then I was off again. When you are wet and cold I find it best to keep going, it keeps you warm somehow. The very dull and drowsy day made the landscape look dull. Most people would have hated being there but through my and my team's eyes it was superb. John was feeding me a sandwich in the rain at dinner as we just looked round at the landscape and he said in a soft voice, 'gorgeous, isn't it?' I ate dinner kneeling up behind our box trailer. The trailer was where we cooked and ate. It was tidy and clean when we started but now it was getting that lived-in look.

When I arrived at the 100 mile rest stop the Union Flag was flying. We had a team photo with a background of small lakes and streams, fed by the glaciers either side of us. We were getting somewhere.

The weather changed on my last five miles of the day to blue sky and sun. On the last stretch the track became rough and rocky and my right hand started to be a problem. It wasn't used to long periods of rough treatment holding the handlebar. It was more than sore skin, the bones felt sore as well. When I reached the camp we thought of an idea to fit a strap onto the right handlebar so that my right hand would hold the strap to steer instead of the handlebar. This would hopefully stop it from getting any worse. We had some straps tying down the food barrels on the roofrack, and so cut a spare one up and fitted it to the handlebar using strong tape. I tested it by riding around the camp.

Later in the evening the sun was strong and very low; there was no wind and no sound either. Everyone was relaxed, doing their own thing. John and I were playing around with cameras in the low sunlight. Dianne went for a walk, Stuart and Andrea listened to music in the Land Rover. The light from the never-ending sun and the lack of sound was amazing, but I found it hard to sleep.

Next morning I was woken by Meat Loaf playing from the Land Rover and a cup of coffee in the door of the tent, what a team! It was a bright sunny day, no wind, perfect. I drank the coffee, lying in my sleeping bag, looking out into the desert. John started to take the tent down, time to get up! The plan for today was to reach the only campsite in the desert, about thirty miles away. We were hoping for a shower.

The trike was going well even though the track was very rough in some parts. Suddenly Stuart and Andrea appeared on foot along side me, then I saw the Land Rover. Thinking they had stopped for a walk, I went on past them. A few miles later I realised that they had stopped at the first five miles, it came so quick that I did not realise. It was a long ten miles to the next rest stop.

The Land Rover was parked by the first river on the trek. I stopped at the back of the trailer and was loaded into it. John was in the trailer with the video camera.

'Close the back,' I said.

'Your wheels are locked and it's not deep, it's good for the shot,' John said.

'Fuck the shot, the trike will slide.'

'It won't, I will hold on to you.'

The trike bounced in the air four times, at the other side my back wheels were an inch from the edge of the trailer!

John stayed in the trailer and filmed some tracking shots of me for about two miles. I suddenly looked up and saw John's bare arse, he had got bored and decided to do a moony at me! Five minutes later Stuart appeared clinging onto the side of the trailer and he climbed along the side then jumped into the back where John was sitting, giving him a shock. This was all happening on a moving trailer on a bumpy track.

I finally arrived at the dinner time rest stop. Dianne had been cooking! Hot potato pancakes and baked beans! Good food, good weather and fantastic scenery. Mmm!

At the twenty-five mile rest stop of the day, Stuart said the campsite should be five miles away, but at the thirty mile stop we still had not reached it.

'It's another five miles,' said Stuart, 'the drinks are on me if it's not.' It wasn't. After thirty-five miles Stuart said, 'I swear it's two miles from here.' Five miles later I arrived at the campsite! I was greeted by John saying 'The price is £4 per tent and there are no showers! Do you want to stay?' For that price you get grass to camp on and a flushing loo, both of which we were not too bothered about. We could go further, then camp in the desert for free. We thought about it but decided to stay, we had done forty miles and we were ready to stop.

The campsite was windy. Stuart and Andrea were cooking dinner. Dianne, John and I sat out of the wind in the tent, eating biscuits that John's girlfriend Loraine had packed him. Andrea did her best but she was turning out to be not much good at cooking. At the last drink before bed Stuart poured some of his brandy into our coffees as the drinks were on him for underestimating the mileage that day!

The next day was a rest day. We were running low on fuel for the trike and the Land Rover and the nearest fuel station was sixty miles north, just out of the desert. We carried five jerry cans of fuel, two for diesel for the Land Rover, two for 4 star for the trike and one for unleaded for the cooker. Stuart and Andrea volunteered to drive the sixty miles to fuel up and get some fresh milk and bread.

While Stuart and Andrea set off early to get the fuel, John, Dianne and I just mellowed out. John gave me the map.

'There is another track we could take which will go through Askja then it will point us in a straight line to the end,' he said.

I had visited Askja on my last trip to Iceland. The immense fifty kilometre square Askja caldera is as remote as things come in Iceland. Cold, windy and forbidding, the site also provides ample evidence of the creative power of nature. The cataclysm that formed the original caldera happened in 1875, when debris ejected from the volcano made a mess as far away as mainland Europe. Activity continued over the next thirty years, culminating in another massive collapse of surface material. This new depression subsequently filled with water and, with a depth of 217 metres, is now the deepest lake in Iceland. Although the lake - a striking sapphire blue - remains frozen most of the year, a smaller and newer crater inside it is still hot and perfect for swimming.

To take John's route would mean being longer on the desert track. The trike was going well but I didn't want to take the piss out of it by doing more on the rough track then we had to. This was only my gut reaction, although it would almost certainly do it, I had studied this alternative route for months at home and I was unsure about changing my mind now.

Half an hour later John came into the tent where I was writing up my diary. He had been talking to the warden at the campsite who said the route to Askja was closed because of the late summer. The route that we were doing had only been opened two weeks before! John asked her if there were cliffs at Hraunhafnartangi where we were finishing the trek and she assured him that there were no cliffs and we would be able to get the trike onto the beach for the finish. She also wished me luck!

We spent the afternoon waiting for Stuart and Andrea to arrive back and watching tour buses come and go. The campsite was the only stop the buses made through the desert. We took the piss out of the tourists when they climbed out of the bus with their video cameras constantly jammed up to their eyeballs. The bravest walked fifty yards from the bus but then the wind got to him, sending him running back to the comfort of the bus. Each of us vowed that we would never reach so low a point in our lives that we even considered going on a coach holiday.

Chapter Six

At 4pm Stuart and Andrea returned with the fuel. We had to move camp or pay for another night at the campsite. By 4.30pm I was on my own again on the trike. The others went ahead to find a camp. I was about to cross a small stream but took the wrong route through it and got stuck in mud. Great. I was not ready for this today, it was supposed to be a rest day, after all! The mud was like a bog, the trike had big balloon tyres and did not get stuck like this very often. I just sat there, the others had just gone so it would be at least an hour before they would come back to look for me. I needed a pee but I couldn't get off the trike because of the deep mud.

Suddenly a truck came round the corner and saw I was in trouble. When you are driving through the desert everyone is ready to help one another. They stop automatically to ask if everything's OK. He towed me slowly out. I thanked him and got going again. I soon arrived at the Land Rover which was waiting by a river for me. They knew I had got stuck because the truck driver stopped and told them. I sat in the Land Rover to cross the river and then carried on my journey on the trike until the ten mile rest stop.

The wind had not stopped for two days now. The left side of me was covered in sand and dirt. My nose and my left ear were full of grit. I sat in the trailer out of the wind for ten minutes during the rest stop. Andrea was convinced there was no wind further on where we could camp. I wasn't convinced. Five miles later I arrived at Camp Loner, as we named it. The Land Rover and trailer were parked in an L shape, as a wind break, the tents were pitch snugly inside the L shape and to finish it off the Union flag was put up in between the Land Rover and trailer. There was nothing but flat desert to the horizon with low sunlight lighting up the golden sand.

Putting up tents was interesting in the high wind. John said something about a blow job, it was one of his cheap jokes. Dianne was cooking in the trailer with a beer. It was cold. Dianne had a circulation problem, her hands would go numb very quickly when it got cold. She fell in love with my big sailing jacket. When I wasn't using it, it would be on Dianne's back. As the sun got lower in the sky our shadows were never-ending. We ate dinner in the tents out of the wind and the grit. Pudding was cake and custard, it tasted amazing, especially in those conditions.

'Dianne,' John shouted, 'JB wants to know what the crunchy bits in the custard are.'

'It's custard à la grit!'

This was the second night we saw the moon in one direction and the sun in the other.

I was happy with the progress we were making. I was pleased with the team but there was still a lot of tension between them and it felt like it was getting worse. They kept it from me but John and Dianne were getting pissed off with Stuart and Andrea. It was a personality clash more then anything. From my point of view I was pleased with the way they were coping with the desert, making tea and meals, putting up tents - all in a gale with sand blowing everywhere. Most people would have cracked up by now.

And most people would say 'why are you doing this? This is not normal!' But this is what I do, I talk to people who do this kind of thing, to me, this is normal. It has become part of my life and I don't think it will ever go away. My family and friends have accepted that this is what I do. Much the same way as Chris Bonnington and Rannulph Finnes' family and friends have.

It just happens that I am disabled. I can imagine that I would be doing similar things if I wasn't disabled.

I awoke with freezing feet the next morning. The wind was still up. I got on the track wearing my big jacket, gloves, a balaclaver and Dianne's sunglasses to keep the sand out of my eyes. It was about forty miles to the end of the desert. I wasn't sure whether I wanted to get out of the desert or not, I loved it so much, but it would be good to see some green grass again away from the grit. The weather had been good to us. In these parts the weather can be a nightmare: snowstorms or sandstorms. It's a dangerous place to be if the weather is bad.

I had quite a lot of buses and Land Rovers pass me on the first five miles and pulled over to the side of the track to let them pass. The team were looking at me through the binoculars, all they could see was a cloud of dust coming slowly towards them.

I pulled in at the five mile stop, very wind-swept but not too cold. The sun lit up the landscape of glaciers behind us. I sat on the trike out of the wind alongside the trailer, and drank tea. '158.9 miles, wwooo!' John shouted as he jumped out of the Land Rover. I got on my way, eager to get as far as possible to the edge of the desert that day so we could get into Akureyri the day after and have a couple of days' rest and a clean up in the town before the final leg to the finish, about 130 miles away. I arrived at the Land Rover by another river crossing. Before we crossed we had some lunch parked on a dried-up river bed. There was a long path of ice to the left of us. This was because of the late summer. Normally the ice would have melted by now and the river would be full.

After we crossed the river (our last crossing of the trek) I got going, climbing high. There were spectacular views over the desert plain with mountains, lakes and glaciers in the background. I kept crossing small streams, and after twenty-five miles, I was thinking about going on and doing thirty-five or forty miles that day. I spotted the Land Rover up on a hill, then suddenly the trike ground to a halt, the engine was running but there was no drive. There was a horrible highpitched scream from the gearbox. A terrible thought ran through my brain, the gearbox, we cannot fix the gearbox, we could fix anything else but not the gearbox because it was sealed with the hydraulic drive. I had tried to find a spare one for the trip but had failed.

A bus stopped, I handed my note to the driver and pointed to the Land Rover on the hill. I got off the trike and saw the Land Rover already on its way, they must have seen me stop. John and Stuart arrived, they left the trailer with the girls back up on the hill. A positive thought ran through my head, OK, maybe it's not the gearbox, it might be something simple like the drive belt had come loose.

Stuart opened the back of the trike and said, 'what do you reckon?' I looked at him in silence. He started the engine, it still sounded horrible. We switched it off quickly. Both of us were mechanically minded and we did not like that noise! We spent fifteen minutes checking the obvious things but it was in my mind and now in Stuart's that we were in trouble. John went back to pick up the trailer and the girls from the hill.

We all sat around in a daze for about twenty minutes: we weren't ready for this one! I sat on my own for a while trying to get my head together, trying to make some sensible decisions. I knew that the trike could not be fixed in Iceland. It did not take long before I had made up my mind that I would come back next year with a new trike to finish the trek. I had my sponsors to think about as well as John's film and my book to finish. Thoughts quickly turned to Ffyona's walk through Africa, she was stopped by a war half way through her walk. She flew back home until the war ended eighteen months later, then returned and continued her walk.

We marked the spot where I had stopped with red tape on a rock and marked the spot on the map as well. I would return and continue my journey from here. We took photographs and then loaded the trike into the trailer, it was a sad sight!

We decided to drive north out of the desert to a campsite to have a clean up and to think about things. Nobody said a lot as we entered civilisation, none of us wanted to be there. We found a campsite near a waterfall, Goodafoss, drove in and pitched our tents on soft green grass at the back of the field. It was about 10.30pm, there was a blue sky and sun. We started cooking dinner, everything was covered in volcanic dust from the desert. Everyone was beginning to relax and slowly adjust to our new situation. Jokes started flying around, we had a beer. Who is first in the shower, then? I was the third one in the shower, it was cold, typical. Why was it cold when you've got boiling hot water coming out of the ground just outside? Maybe it's the same reason why that gearbox had to finally pack up on an expedition but not in my back garden at home.

Next morning the plan was to go into Akureyri. The woman who ran the campsite knew of a mechanic in the town who might be able to fix the trike. I thought this was unlikely but decided to go anyway. Akureyri is Iceland's northern capital, and was about twenty-five miles from the campsite. We packed up and left.

It was a clear day. I sat in the back of the Land Rover looking out of the window, deep in thought about the return trip to carry on the trek. It would make a great story, anyway, I thought, and hoped that my sponsors would understand and cough up some more cash. I wanted to arrive back in England with a very positive attitude to face the sponsors and the press, to make them realise that it is OK to fail and to try again.

We arrived in Akureyri and found the workshop recommended by the campsite woman. As it was a Friday afternoon the mechanic was not interested in our problem.

We drove into town and found a café where we had fresh coffee and sandwiches. This was very different from the desert, we all felt uneasy.

'Let's go to the tourist information centre,' someone said. 'It's just down the road; there might be a disabled centre around and we might be able to borrow a trike or something, they must have something like your trike in this country.'

Chapter Seven

The tourist information centre was a modern building and I spotted a clean modern disabled loo which I used while the others were queuing up.

I came out of the loo and sat at a table covered with maps.

John came up to me and said, 'How about a horse?'

I looked at him, remembering our last trip to Iceland where we tried to go horse riding. I was held by the rider who sat behind me on the saddle; I sat on the horse's neck. Within five minutes I had to get off the horse because I was in pain: I was off sex for at least two months after that day!

John must have known what flashed through my mind because he quickly said, 'You'll have a special saddle.'

I looked at him again. 'Fuck, you are serious, aren't you?'

'Well, they have rung a bloke who has horses, he will be here in five minutes.'

Just then a tall blond bloke walked in, shook my hand and said, 'Hi, I'm Baldvin, what's the plan?' We briefly told him what we were doing.

We got some detailed maps out and showed him the spot where I broke down.

'It is very important we start from that spot,' I said.

Baldvin nodded. 'I understand, no problem.'

I sank back in my chair and thought, this bloke is madder then me, he hasn't said that word 'WHY' yet!

'Meet me at my house at 6pm,' he said. 'You can camp in my garden.'

When Baldvin had gone we sat round the table and looked at each other. '£500 at the most,' said John, guessing what all this would cost. 'Well, that is cheaper than a return trip! It will be an fantastic story for the film and your book. OK, you're not going to be in control like on the trike but you are still crossing Iceland at the same speed.' I did not say much. We walked though the town, it hadn't sunk in yet what I was about to try and do, jokes started flying around about horses.

We got to Baldvin's place just before 6pm. It was a one story house standing on its own. The nearest neighbour was about a mile away. There were horses tied up by the front door.

'Baldvin is not in yet,' said Sigrun, Baldvin's wife. 'I am just taking a group horse riding, but please help yourself to coffee, Baldvin has told me about you, you can camp over there.'

We set up the camp and cooked dinner as normal. We were invited in that night to plan the trip. The major problem was my saddle.

'We need to build one,' said Baldvin.

'What about the seat on the trike?' John said.

'Yes, that would be good,' I said, 'It has an arm and a back rest, and a seat belt.'

As Dianne, John and I lay in our sleeping bags in our tent, I said to John, 'I hope he will not do us for money now he has got us here.' We lay in silence, then John did a impression of a horse which made all three of us crack up.

When I awoke the next morning the seat was already off the trike and sitting on the grass; Stuart had been at work! The expedition was now out of our hands and in Baldvin's. It was Saturday and nothing could be done on the saddle until Monday when the workshops were open in town; things were now out of our hands and we just had to put up with it.

The household was very laid back and friendly. Baldvin had three children. The oldest boy, Thorri, was nineteen and from Baldvin's first marriage. Snedis is the middle child, he was eight when we met him, and the youngest was a girl, Haraldur, who was five. The kids were very independent. In the summer, when there is twenty-four hours of daylight, Icelanders rarely have a proper night's sleep. They are still up working and kids playing outside at one in the morning. The opposite happens in the winter when they have about four or five hours of sunlight a day. They just eat, sleep and bonk.

In today's Iceland close to 90 percent of the population still has the traditional name system while the rest have family names like in Europe (a great deal of those are derived from Norwegian and Danish people who came to Iceland over the last two centuries). Baldvin attempted to explain the name system to me one night.

This is how it works: a newborn child takes its father's first name as its last name. Males receive the -son ('son') ending and females the -dóttir ('daughter') ending.

In some (very rare) cases the children are named after their mother, in which case the rules above are applied unchanged (-son and -dóttir).

Some examples:

A female, Laufey, daughter of Valgeir, is Laufey Valgeirsdóttir

Her brother, Helgi, is then Helgi Valgeirsson.

A couple named Jónas Sveinsson and Elín Karlsdóttir have twins, a boy and a girl. They christen them Hans and Sveinborg respectively, then they are referred to as Hans Jónasson and Sveinborg Jónasdóttir.

The surnames in Iceland are not really names as such but rather patronymics, referring to the father. For this reason Icelanders are never referred to by their last names. Foreigners may find it a bit offensive to be addressed on a first name basis by a total stranger, but that is just Icelandic custom.

In many of the Viking Sagas you can see lines like this one '...there came the warlord Grímur Jónsson Guðmundssonar Ólafssonar Guðmundssonar from the north with his men.' This seems like I am making all this up, but it took me ages to understand!

The storytellers included a little history and family traces in the plot as a comprehensive knowledge of your entire family history was vital in ancient Iceland. Also you needed to know a great deal about almost any other family in Iceland as offending the wrong person could greatly reduce your life expectancy.

The next two days were spent route planning. Baldvin seemed to know almost everyone in

Iceland! He called a friend of his, Arni Logi. 'He is an expert on the area where we will be riding,' said Baldvin. That night Arni Logi turned up. He was a well built Icelander with a constant smile on his face, but he spoke little English. He drove a Mitsubishi Shogun which had four aerials on its roof and was full of electronic gadgets, phones, faxes, navigation equipment and a TV. We worked out that the trip would take about ten days to complete. We also needed about five days to get everything ready, such as the saddle which needed to be built and tried and tested for a start, never mind anything else! I got the feeling that everyone seemed to think that the trip was definitely going to happen. But I thought differently. When I am comfy on that bloody saddle then the trip will be on, I thought, but in the back of my mind I knew that the trip was on whatever happened. We needed to go for it within five days if we had any hope of completing the ten day trip before our plane left from Reykjavik.

Arni Logi would use the five days to recce our route in his car. The route was to be mostly off road so it was important to recce it first to know what was ahead and to have a safe straight through-route.

After the weekend we drove into Akureyri with my seat to a welder Baldvin knew. They talked in Icelandic about how to build the saddle while we stood and watched, trying to get bits of the conversation to understand what the hell was happening.

We chased around to different parts of the town picking up bits for the saddle. Baldvin obviously knew what he was doing but sometimes we did not have a clue, which got us down a bit.

While all this was happening the bad vibe between Andrea and Stuart and Dianne and John got worse. Ever since we had stopped at Baldvin's, Stuart and Andrea slowly lost interest in the expedition, saying they were bored not doing anything. They never complained to me, it was always to John or Dianne. John and Dianne were getting pissed off and upset by their attitude. I couldn't understand it either. They where in Iceland on a free trip, staying in a Icelandic home with some of the most friendly people you ever wished to meet and they still had the balls to complain!

On the Wednesday, John, Dianne, Baldvin and I went into town. We understood from Baldvin that the trip would cost approximately £2000! He asked me to give him half now and I could send the rest when I got home. We went to the bank and cashed £1000.

We then went to the welders and picked up the saddle, then drove to a saddle maker, who fitted all the straps to strap it to the horse. The whole thing looked a very professional job. When we tried the saddle on a horse at a local stables, we found it needed modifying because a bar was pressing on the horse.

The local and national press wanted to interview us so we went on a tour of the press offices. Baldvin gave an interview on the local radio which we heard on the Land Rover's radio on the way back to the house. I thought to myself, this is crazy, I hadn't sat on the bloody horse yet, let alone said 'yes, I'll do it!'

That night Arni Logi phoned saying that he was halfway across our route and there was snow on the ground! 'Oh great!' I muttered, eating my tea.

The next day we collected the modified saddle from the welders and went to the stables in town again where photographers from the newspapers were waiting. The saddle needed more modifying but I sat on the horse for two minutes while the photographers got what they wanted.

I was awoken early the next morning by Baldvin hitting me with three national newspapers which each had a massive photograph on the front page of me sitting on a horse. I looked at the front page - 'oh shit,' - then rolled over back to sleep.

The next few days were spent getting things ready. A big horse box and food and equipment for the horses had to be got. We were induced to the two horses that Baldvin had chosen for my trip: Skjoni and Loki. He told us there were right for the job. They were old and wise, nothing would bother them, they have seen it all. Skjoni was to be my horse. He was brown with white patches, his back was wide, which was good for my saddle to sit on. Skjoni also had a chilled out look permanently on his face, which I liked. Loki was light brown and looked very fit, he was my back-up horse to give Skjoni a rest.

The first horses were brought to Iceland by Viking settlers from Norway around 900 A.D. The Vikings brought the horses with them in their longships. Since there was limited space on the ships for such a long journey, the Vikings took only the best horses with them. Thus the Icelandic breed of horses got a very good start.

*Dinner on the floor
of the desert*

Camp Loner

Coming up to a rest stop at last!

Dianne relaxing after making dinner

Go away and take that bloody horse with you!

Dianne and Baldvin trying to look cool!

Baldvin riding Loki and me trying to
stay on Skjoni!

The ever growing expedition convoy

Dianne leading Loki with Andrea holding my saddle

The team at the finish with a few extras.

Nice day for it!

Me and Baldvin sat behind Edward's 101

Dinner in the middle of nowhere at midnight

Going well on the desert track

A river crossing

Taking the desert by storm!

The horse has since played a vital role in the survival of the Icelandic people for over 1000 years. The Icelandic horse has remained purely bred, and no foreign breed has ever been introduced to Iceland in over 800 years.

There is a long tradition of horse training and competitions in Iceland and there are many annual shows where they compete in racing and other sports. As well as the usual four gaits of walking, trotting, cantering and galloping, the Icelandic horse has a fifth: the tolt. The Icelandic horse has adapted well to the harsh conditions of the Icelandic climate, and horses frequently roam free during the winter, when cattle cannot survive.

We finally got the seat back on the Friday afternoon after more modifications. I got on Skjoni for the first time at 12.30am Saturday. We were leaving at 8am later that morning to drive back into the desert to start the trek. I had a ten minute ride on Skjoni - this was my first and only test ride! Everyone was there, the whole family, friends, people from the next village and Arni Logi and Peter. Peter was a Swiss guy of about twenty-five, who stayed and worked for Baldvin for the summer. He would be coming and helping for the first part of the trip.

It felt a bit strange sitting so high and with no control over the four legged beast, but everything felt OK. It was too late to have second thoughts, the only thing do to do now was to go for it and see what happened! By one in the morning everything was all set for the second stage of my journey.

Chapter Eight

The next morning Skjoni and Loki were collected from their grazing ground and loaded into the horse box, which would be towed by Baldvin in his Land Rover. We would go ahead and meet Baldvin and Peter at the start point in the desert.

We arrived at the start point first: Baldvin would take a while as he had to drive slowly with the horse box over the rough desert track. We made a brew and sat around, it was nice to be back.

Baldvin finally arrived, he was not happy, we were further into the desert than he expected and he was worried about water for the horses.

We had two jerry cans of water and a trailer full of hay.

Baldvin had dropped Peter off further up the track with Loki. The saddle was put on Skjoni by my start line. I was off, I had my trek back! The time had amazingly got to 4pm before we started. We had to get to a lake at the end of the desert some fifteen miles away to camp so that the horses could drink.

Dianne walked at the side of me holding the saddle, which was not perfect yet.

The speed was very slow compered to my trike. We only covered three miles in a hour instead of five. At the first three mile rest stop I realised that I had a problem: not my back, as I had feared, but my head and neck. With the movement of the horse, my head was constantly rocking back and forth very violently, there was no way I could stop it. The seat did not help as the back rest was very loose. During the rest stop Stuart tried to tighten the back rest up but it was old and worn. The rest stops were very long, thirty to forty minutes, so that the horses could rest. This made progress even slower.

The next three miles I was on Loki. We did not keep to the track, just went cross-country to cut some miles off. The Land Rovers had difficulty keeping up with us. Andrea was walking beside me, she loved horses and was now in her element. My head was rocking worse than ever; if I looked up, my sight was a blur, I couldn't focus on anything. We were crossing some amazing country, rough rocky terrain that I wouldn't take a Land Rover through never mind a bloody horse that I wasn't in control over!

Four hours later, through my dodgy eyesight I spotted the lake that marked the end of the day. I shouted out as no one else could see it - I was higher then everyone. Two hours later we still hadn't reached the lake, it was 11.30pm and I and every one else have had enough, I was in pain from my neck and my head. We loaded the horses into the horse box, having decided to start again from here the next day, and drove to the camp. I felt like shit. My right eye was swollen and painful, probably because a blood vessel in my eye had swollen. I had a headache and my neck was not too good either.

I sat in my tent with John and Dianne and said to them I was really worried about doing some permanent damage to myself.

'Just say the word and just stop, it's not worth doing damage to your health,' Dianne said.

By 1am we were eating dinner in our tents looking over the lake. I decided that if I felt better in the morning I would carry on and see what happened.

'Anyway, today was the first time you have been on a horse,' said John, sitting cross-legged in the tent eating. 'Most people are sore after their first time on a horse, but most people's ride for the first time is just for half an hour, not fucking seven hours - you mad sod!'

I woke the next morning without any pain in my eye, although I'd fully expected it. I talked to John before we got up about fitting a strap for my left hand so that I could pull myself up away from the back rest. This might reduce some movement to my head

John and Dianne got up and left me for a while. Baldvin came into the tent and lay beside me.

'Good morning, how do you feel? I can phone Arni Logi today and ask him to go the hospital and get you a neck collar, he can meet up with us tonight, do you think you can carry on until then?'

'Yes,' I stupidly said!

We loaded Skjoni into the box: it took three people to push him in. We left Loki by the camp while we went back to where we had stopped the night before and did the two miles back to the camp. While we were gone the others packed up the camp. Andrea walked beside me while Baldvin led. I felt OK, my head was not rocking too badly. We were coming over the hill which looked over the camp when Loki sensed that Skjoni was getting near. Loki let out a big neigh and Skjoni did the same in reply; they carried on talking to each other until we reached the camp again.

The next three mile stretch was on Loki, the end of the desert was getting near as greenery and lakes started to appear. My head was rocking badly again, it was worse on Loki than on Skjoni. At the next three mile rest stop Edward arrived. Edward was from Holland and was touring around Iceland in his Land Rover 101. He was about 45 years old and a friend of Baldvin's; we had met him at Baldvin's house earlier in the week.

We made a neck collar out of a old sponge cushion, cutting it so it would fit my neck, and tied it with a bandage. It did not work very well after all the effort. I now had three vehicles following me: my Land Rover, Baldvin's Land Rover and now the 101 belonging to Edward (who looked like he was here to stay).

By the dinner time stop we were out of the desert. I did not feel well at all, I had a headache, my eye was hurting a lot again and my sight was blurred. We had a very long dinner time to rest the horses.

Baldvin came up to me with a map. We could save ourselves about five miles by crossing a river just up ahead, he told me. We could ride up to the edge of the river then drive around the river by road and ride off from the other side. Baldvin asked me whether this would fit in with my goals for the expedition.

'Yes it is, it would be the same as a river crossing in the desert.'

I got on Skjoni, Baldvin and John walked me to the river. As we approach the river flies attacked us. Thousands of them were all round our faces, it was too much for me, I just sat there and laughed. We touched the river bank and walked back to the Land Rovers. It was nice just to rest in the passenger seat and listening to music as we drove to the other side of the lake. We had to drive through a farm to get to the lake; of course, Baldvin knew the farmer! We could also camp at the farm overnight.

I touched the bank on the other side of the lake on Skjoni, Baldvin and Andrea walked me across some fields to the farm. By the time we arrived Arni Logi was there, he brought three neck collars, one of them fitted snugly. We set up camp, Baldvin and Peter went home which was not far away. We had not done too many miles today. The team was getting irritable because we were making slow progress and we were not in control of the journey now, as we had been with the trike. It was Baldvin who was making all the decisions now. We had to change from using a toolbox and WD40 to hay, saddles and above all, an understanding of horses!

I had a beer with Dianne while she was making dinner in the trailer. She had the same sense of humour as me, very very strange!

Chapter Nine

Baldvin and Peter arrived at about ten the next morning. Edward would find us later in the day, Baldvin told us.

Up to now Baldvin had been leading my horse by walking but the plan was that once me and the horse had got used to each other, Baldvin would try to lead by riding the spare horse. Eventually we set off, the neck collar worked really well. Going up the hill out of farm I was on Skjoni and Baldvin on Loki, Peter walked behind us in case we ran into problems. Skjoni wasn't happy, he kept stopping: my saddle must have been rubbing him again. We adjusted the saddle and carried on. One of the Land Rovers went ahead and the other one behind to look out for cars that were going fast and tell them to slow down, as fast cars would frighten the shit out of the horses.

A few miles up the road Skjoni stopped again. The saddle needed more adjustment. There was a farm further up the road that Baldvin knew had a workshop. We stopped and Baldvin, Peter and Stuart drove to the farm to sort the saddle out.

I sat in the Land Rover with Dianne and John. I wasn't feeling too good again, this time it was my stomach, I hadn't been to the loo for days. I just needed a clean loo and everyone to piss off for an hour! John fed me a yoghurt: 'Dianne said this might help you!'

The others arrived back having done what was needed with the farm's welding equipment, including welding the backrest so it was solid. We continued on and my stomach settled down. We were heading into Myvatn where we would stay that night. The week that we stayed at Baldvin's the weather was very cold and it rained all most every day, but the three days we had been riding the weather had been excellent: blue sky, sun and quite warm.

Peter took over from Baldvin leading on Loki, we went across country on off-road tracks. Peter and I tried some trotting, it felt good as my head didn't rock half as much. But: 'trotting was bad for my saddle as it might hurt Skjoni,' Baldvin told us at the next rest stop. Peter and I looked at each other and shrugged our shoulders, well, we enjoyed it anyway.

While the others were resting in their Land Rovers, Stuart and I had a peeing competition. Stuart had an amazing bladder, he could pee nonstop for five or six minutes! This made my thirty-six seconds look pathetic. While this was going on Edward arrived and everyone got out to meet him, walking around Stuart and me, not realising what we had got in our hands!

We got going again, this was the last three miles of the day. Baldvin led on Loki and Andrea was walking beside me because the track was now getting rough. Edward had came through this way to meet us. He said it was very scary in his 101! Baldvin suddenly cracked up, looking at the track. 'WHAT, this is too rough for his Land Rover? What a prat!' Baldvin told us that Edward, even though he was about forty-five, still lived with his mum back in Holland. He expected dinner to be on the table at a certain time. His pride and joy was his Land Rover 101, which he kept spotlessly clean. The Land Rover 101 was built for the army, it is capable of doing far more than Edward's wildest dreams, which were turning out to be not that wild! Poor bloke!

Skjoni suddenly stopped, my saddle needed adjusting again. Stuart jumped out to help me off Skjoni, so that Baldvin could rearrange the saddle.

We got to the end of the last three miles of the day and drove into Myvatn and found a campsite and a loo!!! Edward stayed with us and followed us wherever we went. Baldvin and Peter went back home with the horses, Baldvin saying that he would meet us at ten the next morning at the start point.

After dinner we went for a drive around Mynatn, this area is amazing: one of the most interesting and spectacular places in Iceland. The variety of scenery is remarkable - mountains, lavafields, solfatara fields, deserts and moraines. With an area of 38 km², it is the third largest lake in Iceland and was formed some 3800 years ago by the damming effect of a lava flow. Mynatn is the second highest inhabited part of Iceland (277m) and as well as farming, the local people now have some industry based on utilising the geothermal energy.

The geothermal heat comes from local active sources and there have been recent eruptions that have produced lava. Any warnings about possible eruptions must therefore be taken seriously and for those who wish to make a quick exit, the airstrip is on a large flat terrace above the campsite!

Next morning we met Baldvin, he had left Peter to help with work back at home. By now my team and I had learnt a lot about the horses and could now help. Therefore, there was no need for Peter to be around. This was a shame in a way because I was getting to know him and I really liked him.

Baldvin had also left Skjoni to rest for the day. Skjoni's replacement was a mare, Emma. She was frisky and very powerful. Baldvin led me by walking, Andrea walked beside me holding my saddle as it was not perfect by any means on Emma, though my head stayed absolutely still. It was the most comfortable ride since this epic began! John was riding Loki, Dianne was driving Baldvin's Land Rover behind us and Edward was following Stuart who was in my Land Rover up ahead.

We got to the end of the track and joined Road 1, heading east for a while. John was now leading on Loki as we rode along Road 1. We passed a farm which had horses and this sent our horses mad. I was shitting myself. We were on a steamy main road, John had not much experience with horses, never mind controlling two at the same time! We walked slowly on, trying to keep control and stay calm. We really wanted to kick the shit out of the horses but we thought it might not go down too well! Luckily, we were soon off Road 1 and back on a track heading north again.

After dinner, Stuart and Andrea took over. I was on Loki, Stuart was leading on foot and Andrea was holding the saddle. Halfway through the three miles the saddle had to be adjusted again. We were heading towards Kraffla which is a highly volcanic area, it last erupted in 1984. I muttered, 'if this horse is frightened of a car horn, I wonder what the fucker would do if that erupted now?'

Stuart looked up at me. 'You don't like horses do you?'

'Nar,' I said.

At the rest stop I wasn't feeling great, my head had been rocking again and all of us were feeling knackered. I knelt on the road by the trailer and touched the road, it was really hot, we really were in a highly volcanic area. All three vehicles were parked in a row at the side of the road along with two trailers: it was a long convoy. Everyone had a mug of coffee in one hand and a butty in the other and was either sitting resting on food tubs in the trailer, on wheel arches or in their cabs looking into space. We were a team, we were there doing something very special and very real. I lent up against the 101 to shelter from a light shower and wondered how the hell I could better this feeling.

All too soon there was action, the rest stop was over. Everyone got up to prepare to move on. My saddle was put on Loki, my collar and helmet was put on me. Stuart picked me up and carried me over onto my saddle, put my seat belt on, then we walked off. Baldvin led on foot and Dianne walked beside me. It was getting hot as the rain cloud cleared and the sun came out. The convoy passed us, onto the next rest stop. We fell silent and just walked. I was uncomfortable, my neck was score and I started to get a friction burn on one side of my chin from the collar. I was getting very pissed off with my helmet, it kept coming loose and coming over my eyes and banging my head. With all the discomfort I did not need this as well!

The last three miles of the day were with John and Dianne. We were now walking away from Myvatn and into a desert again. Baldvin went ahead, Arni Logi was meeting us at a rescue hut up ahead. We arrived at the hut relieved that it was the end of the day.

Arni Logi had his maps out. The next two days we were to ride across the longest valley in the country on very rough tracks, sometimes there would be no tracks at all.

Baldvin was going home for the night, he would take Emma back and bring Skjoni with him in the morning. This would be the last time he would go home before we got to the end of the expedition.

Edward went off with Arni Logi to have a look at the first part of the next day's route. Edward had left his keys in his 101, Stuart shouted, 'JB, fancy a quick ride?'

'Yar, I have been hinting all week to have a ride but the git took no notice.'

Stuart knew 101s from the army. Edward had done the back out as a camper. It had a bed, cooker and even a bloody table. In the cab was every kind of spare, as you would expect from an army vehicle. Between the driver and the passenger seat there was a bloody great V8 engine to warm you up if you were feeling cold. A four inch rubber hose came out vertically from the engine, then did a 90 degree bend and went out through the dash to the radiator. We did a small tour of the desert before Edward came back and had a heart attack because he saw his vehicle doing more than 30mph!

Arni Logi had got us permission to stay in the rescue hut. The hut was quite small: two rooms with two bunks in each and, above all, CURTAINS! The twenty-four hour daylight was getting to us slightly!

Edward was trying to con us into cooking him some dinner because he said it was his birthday and he had a cold. Mmmhmmm.

It was good to be back in the desert again, we had snow-covered mountains in the distance with an excellent sunset behind them.

Chapter Ten

The next morning the vehicles went off north following a small desert track. Baldvin and I took a short cut and rode straight across the desert.

We eventually joined the track which the Land Rovers had taken. We were coming to the end of the three miles when we heard someone shouting from the top of a hill above us, which startled the horses. It was Stuart.

For the next three miles John took over from Baldvin riding Loki and I was on Skjoni.

'So this is what it's like riding through the desert on your own,' John said.

But we were soon out of the desert and in a lush green landscape. We were following a track which went through bushes and green banks.

Every so often we had to go through gates. John did well controlling two horses and opening and closing gates at the same time. I felt nervous not being in control.

At dinner Edward was onto us again about feeding him but Dianne had him under control! He did not realise that we had just enough food for five people for four weeks and it was now running short, and he had stocks of food in his van. He was just a lazy, selfish git who thought he was doing us a favour by following us.

Baldvin took over from John. We were making good progress, then suddenly saw the vehicles stopped up ahead. There was about a quarter of a mile of ice ahead of them and they were panicking. Baldvin waved at them to keep moving but they had no idea and got stuck half way across. Andrea and Dianne just carried on with me and the horses while Baldvin went and sorted out the boys.

About forty minutes later the vehicle caught up with us. We stopped for a rest and took the piss out of Edward who had yet to emerged from his 101 after the epic with the ice.

My right boot had come to bits so Stuart got the red gaffer tape out and did a quick repair job on it while I laid motionless on the grass.

Anther five miles should make it to the day's end. We were heading to a cottage that Baldvin knew for the night.

I was on Loki for the last leg of the day. Baldvin led on foot and Dianne was riding Skjoni and was trying to look cool because she had not been on a horse in years - she was actually shitting herself.

The last three miles were hard and painful. We got to the cottage, a triangular building used for travellers. It looked very small from the outside but once inside it was really long, with bunks along the sides, a long table down the middle and a kitchen. Some travellers were already there when we arrived. Stuart strolled up to me with a candlestick in his hand and a grin on his face. On closer inspection this turned out to be a highly polished gearbox cog with a candle stuck in it, and there were four or five of them along the table. Stuart and I suddenly cracked up, we could not believe what it was. The travellers looked at us, surprised.

'It's OK,' Stuart said to them, 'we are not mad, but we needed one of these about seventy-five miles down the road.'

The cottage was in a hot spring area. There was hot mud bubbling in one spot and red hot water coming out from the ground: far too hot for a shower. Next to the cottage there was a small shed in the same shape as the cottage. It had a flushing loo which was fed by the hot spring.

Arni Logi was due to arrive that night but we did not know when, it could be anytime because he never slept. About three in the morning the door flew open. 'Hello Hello,' it was Arni Logi. He went upstairs to where Baldvin was sleeping. I was sleeping downstairs and suddenly became aware of somebody by me, it was Sigrun, Baldvin's wife. She was as shocked to see me as I was to see her. She had a day off from horseriding at home and she had come to join us for the next day.

I awoke up early. The area stank of sulphur and it was now making me feel ill and I could not eat breakfast.

We got going, Baldvin and I on our own riding through the green valley. After about two miles we came across the Land Rovers, stuck in deep mud. Edward had no bloody idea and was beginning to be a problem. Stuart had got stuck as well which annoyed him; the wrong attitude to take and very dangerous for the situation. I rode on with the girls while Baldvin sorted out the Land Rovers again. About an hour later the Landrovers caught us up. Stuart drove like a mad man over the rough track which wrecked almost everything in the trailer. I was not happy and Stuart knew about it.

We had a long lunch break while we shorted everything out in the trailer. Then me and John carried on. Once out of the valley we would be on roads until the Arctic sea. I kept seeing glimpses of the sea from the horse but the end was about three days away, I was beginning to get excited!

We finally made it to the end of the valley after a long afternoon ride. Arni Logi was waiting for us to take Sigrun back home. We said our goodbyes and stopped on the road at the last rest stop before the last three or five miles to the campsite at Asbyrgi, where we planned to camp. We were back in civilisation and a crowd had gathered around us, they knew of us from the press. We let Baldvin entertain them, he was good at that!

We got on the road again. The others went to set up camp while Baldvin and I plodded on. Halfway to the campsite Skjoni kept stopping, he was getting pissed off, it had been a long day and this was our twelfth hour on the road. Skjoni was telling us it was time to stop. I transferred from Skjoni to Loki for the final two miles. We finally got to the campsite and stopped at the entrance where John was waiting with the Land Rover. I got into the Land Rover while John helped Baldvin to load the horses into the horse box. John and I drove to the tents while Baldvin took the horses to a nearby paddock. The campsite was full and John and I looked at each other: were we ready to be surrounded by people again? Dinner was on, it was about 10pm. We relaxed with a beer. Baldvin arrived back in a crazy mood. There was a good feeling that evening. Everyone was so knackered that no one gave a shit what they said or did.

The next morning we packed up camp and drove to the entrance of the campsite. A few miles up ahead was a bridge. I was on Loki, Dianne and Andrea were walking with me, together with a dog we had made a fuss of at the campsite, which had now attached itself to us. The others went on ahead to stop the traffic on the bridge. Once over the bridge we walked on the grass verge by the side of the road. Loki was being a pain in the arse. He was very slow, obviously not happy.

We were now heading up the most northeasterly peninsula of Iceland, with about two or three more days to finish the trek to the top of the peninsula. John was following us in the Land Rover, the others were up ahead. I was beginning to suffer a lot of discomfort. My head was rocking a hell of a lot on Loki and someone had made a cock up on the mileage for the rest stop. By the time we reached the Land Rovers we had done six miles instead of three. I was in pain and was not happy. Everyone blamed everyone else for the cock up.

I had about an hour's rest before I carried on. The sun was hot as we got going again. We joined Road 85 which went all the way to our finishing point. The sea was now to our left as the road hugged the peninsula's coastline.

Baldvin had a friend who ran a trout farm a few miles up ahead and he invited us in for a coffee and a look around. It was hot inside and we sat and had fresh smoked salmon and fresh coffee. We let Baldvin do most of the talking. We sat there in a daze, the four week trip was catching up with us and we were absolutely bollocksed.

It was a very big effort to get to back on the horse and carry on, but the end of the expedition was definitely coming close. Yet another twelve hour day - it was 10.30pm as Baldvin and I rode into the village of Kopasker where we were camping. Dianne and John had gone ahead some time before to set up camp and get the dinner on. The village was quiet and sleepy. We spotted the campsite and our orange tents. We settled the horses, sat down and drank coffee. No one said much, there was no need to talk. We ate dinner looking out over the Arctic Ocean.

Chapter Eleven

We had some leftovers from the day before, so we had smoked salmon and real coffee for breakfast!

'Any top hotel in bloody London could not top this breakfast,' said Stuart. Baldvin had the map out.

'We could make it to the end today if we went for it but it would be very late when we got there.'

I said, 'OK, let's camp about ten miles from the end tonight and tomorrow we will do the last ten miles in the morning and get to the end in the afternoon.' Everyone agreed that was best so we could enjoy the finish.

We had another hard day's ride. I was suffering from the rocking but just focused on getting to the end after one more day. Tomorrow, tomorrow, tomorrow, the end is tomorrow.

We had dinner on a beach. Stuart went for a swim in the Arctic sea and by the swearing that he was doing we gathered it was very cold!!

We made it to a very small village and pitched our tents in a field. John made a fire out of driftwood from the beach, and Dianne made dinner out of odd things that we had left from the food barrels and some Smash potato from Edward's food store in his van. Then John and Dianne went to a farm to try to get the batteries charged up for the video camera.

Next morning the horses were very tense and jumpy. They knew this was the final leg. John and I rode off from the camp. He was on Loki and I was on Skjoni. The Land Rovers passed us. Baldvin was going to the farm to organise the press and TV for the finish. He was also interviewed for the midday news on the radio. Meanwhile, John and I were having big problems with Loki. He was definitely going his own way. I was shitting myself. John had to get off twice to control him. If John had lost his grip and let go, Loki would have darted off and Skjoni would have followed with me on his back! We gave Loki a bollocking, saying we would kick his head in if he did not stop acting about! We were not in the mood to be messed around by a sodding horse. John decided to walk Skjoni and we called Dianne over to walk Loki.

At the dinner time stop we had about five miles to go. Arni Logi and his wife arrived. We listened to the midday news on the radio in the Land Rover. A cameraman turned up and interviewed Baldvin and John. We did not know it but we were big news around Iceland. I was probably the first disabled nutter to do this.

I got on Loki, the plan was to swop onto Skjoni for the very last stretch. I suddenly spotted the lighthouse at Hraunhafnartangi - shit, I could see the finish. People started waving from their cars, they must have heard the midday news. I changed onto Skjoni, the last stretch was over a lava field. Another news cameraman was flying in from Reykjavik, as we past the lighthouse I saw him running like hell with his camera along the beach. Suddenly we were there, we had run out of land. We collapsed into the Arctic Ocean. WE HAD MADE IT!

The rest of the team joined us in the sea with Ffyona's champagne. I forgot what happened next but a hot shower and a hot meal at a local hotel springs to mind!

Conclusion

I did a total mileage of 304 miles. Of that, I did 180 miles on the trike and 124 miles on horseback, with my head rocking for most of that 124 miles! I lost count of how many times I thought about giving up because of the discomfort I was in. But you cannot give up when you have got a four vehicle support team behind you! I was lucky I had such a fantastic team! We had done what we set out to do.

After I returned to England, the Royal Geographic Society were holding the very first seminar on 'Disabled Explorers' and they asked me to give a talk on the trip. I was asked back to the RGS a month later to do the same talk at the annual 'Explore 95' seminar where there were about 300 people who were planning their own expeditions.

I lost contact with Andrea and Stuart but no doubt we will get in touch again one day.

John is still doing odd and crazy jobs. I get phone calls from him now and then asking me what I think of some crazy idea he has just had.

Dianne is still studying. In the next few weeks she is flying out to Greenland on a geographic expedition. She is also planning her own expedition to Africa next year. She has got the expedition bug and she blames it on me!

And to me, my neck recovered quickly from that bloody horse. I miss the desert alot, I will go back one day.